THOUSAND OAKS LIBRARY

3 2052 01253 1995

AUG   2016

DISCARD

D0744535

THOUSAND OAKS LIBRARY
1401 E. Janss Road
Thousand Oaks, California

WHAT'S INSIDE?
MODERN MILITARY AIRCRAFT

Aaron R. Murray

PowerKiDS
press™

WHAT'S INSIDE?
MODERN MILITARY AIRCRAFT

Aaron R. Murray

PowerKiDS press™

Published in 2016 by The Rosen Publishing Group, Inc.
29 East 21st Street, New York, NY 10010

Cataloging-in-Publication Data
Murray, Aaron R.
Modern military aircraft / by Aaron R. Murray.
p. cm. — (What's inside?)
Includes index.
ISBN 978-1-5081-4611-7 (pbk.)
ISBN 978-1-5081-4612-4 (6-pack)
ISBN 978-1-5081-4613-1 (library binding)
1. Airplanes, Military — Juvenile literature. I. Murray, Aaron R. II. Title.
UG1240.M88 2016
623.7'46—d23

Copyright © Amber 2016

Project Editor: Michael Spilling
Design: Brian Rust and Andrew Easton
Picture Research: Terry Forshaw

Photographs:
Art-Tech/Aerospace: 6, 7, 8
Dassault Aviation: 34 (K. Tokunaga), 35 (K. Tokunaga), 36 (F. Robineau)
Eurofighter: 30, 31, 32
SAAB Gripen: 22, 23, 24
U.S. Department of Defense: 3, 10, 11, 12, 14, 15, 16, 18, 19, 20, 26, 27, 28, 38, 39, 40, 42, 43, 44

Artworks:
Art-Tech/Aerospace: 9, 13, 17, 21
Military Visualizations Inc.: 1, 25, 29, 33, 37, 41, 45

All rights reserved. No part of this book may be reproduced in any form without permission in writing from the publisher, except by a reviewer.

Manufactured in the United States of America
CPSIA Compliance Information: Batch #BW16PK:
For Further Information contact Rosen Publishing, New York, New York at 1-800-237-9932

j 623.746

Contents

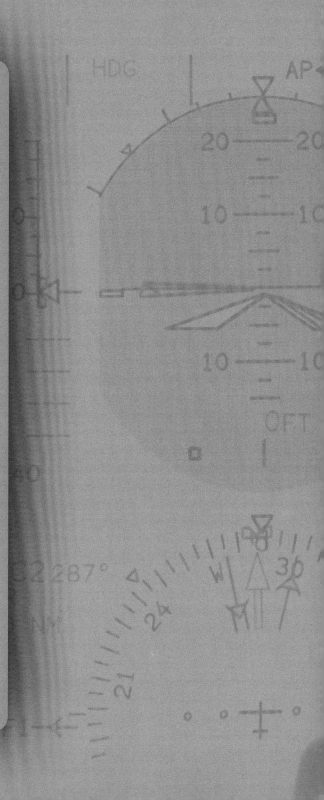

Mirage F1

France was a world leader in jet fighter development after World War II (1939–1945). Her finest warplane was the Mirage III—until the high-performance Mirage F1 appeared.

Although of a similar size to the **delta-winged** Mirage III, the Mirage F1 had twice the range and much greater **agility**.

Fighter of Choice

After its appearance in 1966, this French-built **supersonic** fighter became the main combat aircraft of more than a dozen air forces. The Mirage F1 is designed for air combat and ground attack. More than 720 were built from 1966 to 1992. This single-engine attack fighter has **swept-back wings**

Air-to-air missiles are fixed to the wings and fuselage of this French Mirage F1.

A fully armed Mirage F1 waits on a runway.

high on its **fuselage**. The F1 is armed with two 30 mm (1.18-inch) cannons, as well as ground-attack rockets. Mounted on its wings and fuselage are air-to-air, **anti-ship**, and **laser-guided** missiles.

Did you know?

• Mirage F1 fighters are still important weapons for air forces in Africa and the Middle East, including the countries of Iran, Morocco, Jordan, Kuwait, Qatar, Libya, and South Africa.

• The first Mirage F1 crashed during a test flight in 1966, but France did not give up on developing these fighters.

Anti-Terror Operations

In the mid-1980s, French Mirage F1 fighters fought rebel forces in North Africa. In the early 1990s, they served with an allied force led by the United States against Iraq. In 2013 F1s again attacked rebels and terrorists in North Africa. The Mirage F1's wingspan is 27 feet 6 inches (8.4 m), and it can reach a height of 65,600 feet (20,000 m). Its maximum speed is **Mach** 2.2—or 1,673 miles per hour (2,693 km/h).

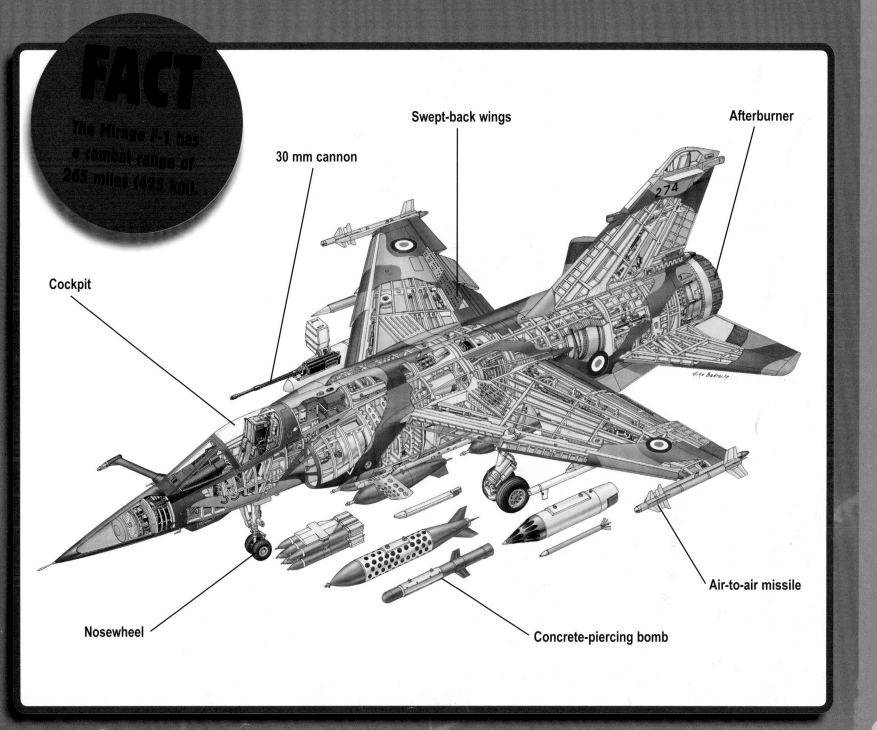

FACT

The Mirage F-1 has a combat range of 265 miles (425 km).

Swept-back wings

Afterburner

30 mm cannon

Cockpit

274

Mike Badrocke

Air-to-air missile

Nosewheel

Concrete-piercing bomb

F-15E Strike Eagle

When the Soviet Union fell in 1991, the U.S. military prepared for the next challenge. The U.S. Air Force wanted fighters that could do more than defeat enemy aircraft. So the F-15E Strike Eagle was developed to win air superiority over the battlefield.

Dogfights and Strike Fighters

The new F-15E Strike Eagle is a **multirole fighter**. It improves upon the earlier F-15 Eagle, which was excellent in **air-to-air combat**, or "dogfights," against other fighters. The F-15E is not only superior in aerial battles but is also effective as a **strike fighter** that can hit targets on the ground.

An F-15 Eagle fires an air-to-air missile during a training exercise.

Did you know?

- **The air forces of Israel, Saudi Arabia, South Korea, and Singapore also have versions of the F-15E.**

- **The F-15E's maximum speed of Mach 2.5—or 1,900 miles per hour (3,060 km/h)—is more than twice the speed of sound.**

fighter jets to protect them on long missions. With a range of 2,400 miles (3,862 km) and a top speed of 1,900 miles per hour (3,060 km/h), the F-15E can hit distant targets and return safely home. The F-15E is armed with a Gatling cannon, as well as air-to-air and air-to-surface missiles. It can deliver both **conventional** and **nuclear** bombs.

Two U.S. F-15E Strike Eagles taxi at Balad Air Base in northern Iraq during the Iraq War (2003–2011).

Introduced by the U.S. Air Force in 1988, the F-15E saw action in Iraq, Afghanistan, Libya, and in the Balkan region of southeast Europe.

All-Weather Fighter

The F-15E can attack day or night and in any weather. Strike aircraft once needed an **escort** of

FACT

The U.S. Air Force currently has more than 200 F-15E fighters in service.

Dorsal airbrake

Twin tail fins

Weapons officer's seat

Pilot's seat

Radar

Mike Badroche

Air-to-surface bomb

Laser-guided bomb

Mikoyan MiG-29 Fulcrum

In 1983 the Soviets introduced the MiG-29, known as the "Fulcrum." The Fulcrum is a multirole fighter. This means it operates as an interceptor of enemy aircraft and as a ground-attack warplane.

The MiG-29 Fulcrum was developed to **counter** new American fighters, such as the F-15 Eagle and the F-16 Fighting Falcon.

A Warplane for Many

MiG-29 Fulcrums can have different designs, weapons, and purposes. Fulcrums were meant to give the Soviets superiority over **NATO** fighter planes and enemy ground defenses.

The MiG-29 has been produced since 1983 and is still being manufactured. More than 1,600 are in use. They serve in the air forces of 30 nations, including Russia, India, Ukraine, Syria, and even some NATO countries. MiG-29s have

Malaysian Air Force Fulcrums maneuver during an air show.

seen action during conflicts in Iraq, Sudan, Ethiopia, and Syria.

Long-Range and Fast

The MiG-29 can carry out long-range operations and can take off and land on short runways, including those of **aircraft carriers**. The MiG-29 was designed for speed and for agility. The MiG-29 is 57 feet (17.4 m) long and has a wingspan of

Did you know?

• **The Soviet Union did not usually name its aircraft. NATO staff gave the MiG-29 the name "Fulcrum-A." Soviet pilots liked the name Fulcrum and used it unofficially.**

• **NATO defended the West against the Soviets, but today some NATO countries buy Fulcrums from Russia. Poland, a member of NATO, has 32 MiG-29 fighter planes.**

37 feet 3 inches (11.4 m). The aircraft can reach a top speed of Mach 2.25—1,711 miles per hour (2,754 km/h). Its range is 880 miles (1,430 km), and it can climb to 59,100 feet (18,013 m). The Fulcrum is armed with a 30-mm (1.18-inch) cannon and air-to-air missiles.

A German air force Fulcrum fires a missile during NATO training exercises.

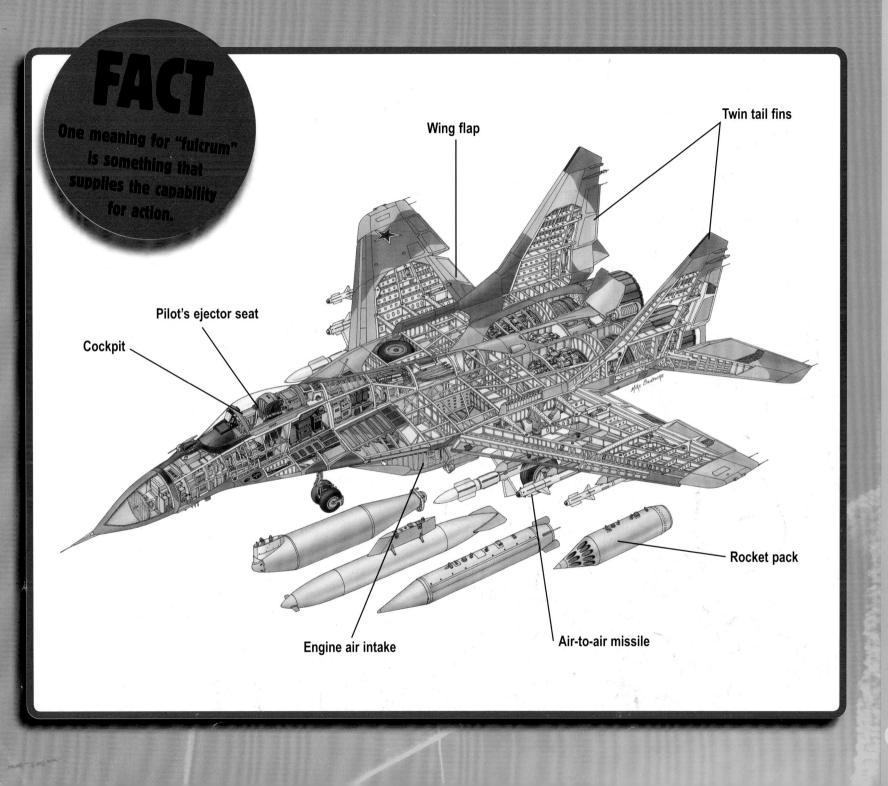

FACT

One meaning for "fulcrum" is something that supplies the capability for action.

Wing flap

Twin tail fins

Pilot's ejector seat

Cockpit

Mike Badrocke

Rocket pack

Engine air intake

Air-to-air missile

Sukhoi Su-27 Flanker

In 1969 the Soviet Union learned of the U.S. F-X fighter program to produce the F-15 Eagle. To counter this challenge, Soviets developed two fighters: the short-range MiG-29 and the longer-range Su-27.

Introduced in 1985, the Su-27 is **supermaneuverable**. Its range of 2,193 miles (3,530 km) made it a good combat partner for the shorter-range MiG-29.

Pride of the Russian Air Force

The Su-27 proved to be an excellent fighter and many versions followed. The Su-30 is a multirole, all-weather fighter with added air-to-surface capability. The Su-33 can be used on aircraft carriers while the Su-34 and Su-35 are enhanced strike fighters. Nine other nations, including the

A Russian Su-27 Flanker lands after a 2011 training exercise with U.S. and Canadian fighters on the west coast of Russia.

People's Republic of China, fly versions of the Su-27. Russia flew Su-27s in wars with Georgian forces in the 1990s and again in 2008.

Superior Speed and Altitude

The Su-27 has a wingspan of 48 feet 3 inches (14.7 m) and is 72 feet (21.9 m) long. The Su-27's capabilities let the pilot perform maneuvers impossible for

A U.S. Marine general (upper right) looks over a Chinese Su-27 Flanker parked at an airfield in China.

most aircraft. It can climb to 62,500 feet (19,000 m), higher than its rival, the MiG-29. With a maximum speed of Mach 2.35 (1,787 mph; 2,876 km/h), the Su-27 is also faster. Armed with a 30-mm (1.18-inch) cannon and air-to-air missiles for fighter combat, the Su-27 can also carry air-to-ground and air-to-ship missiles, as well as laser-guided bombs.

Did you know?

- **Russia's flight exhibition team, the Russian Knights, perform their acrobatic stunts flying in Su-27s.**

- **The Su-27 is the first fighter to perform the "cobra" maneuver. The pilot suddenly slows the plane down, raises its nose to a vertical position, then levels off again.**

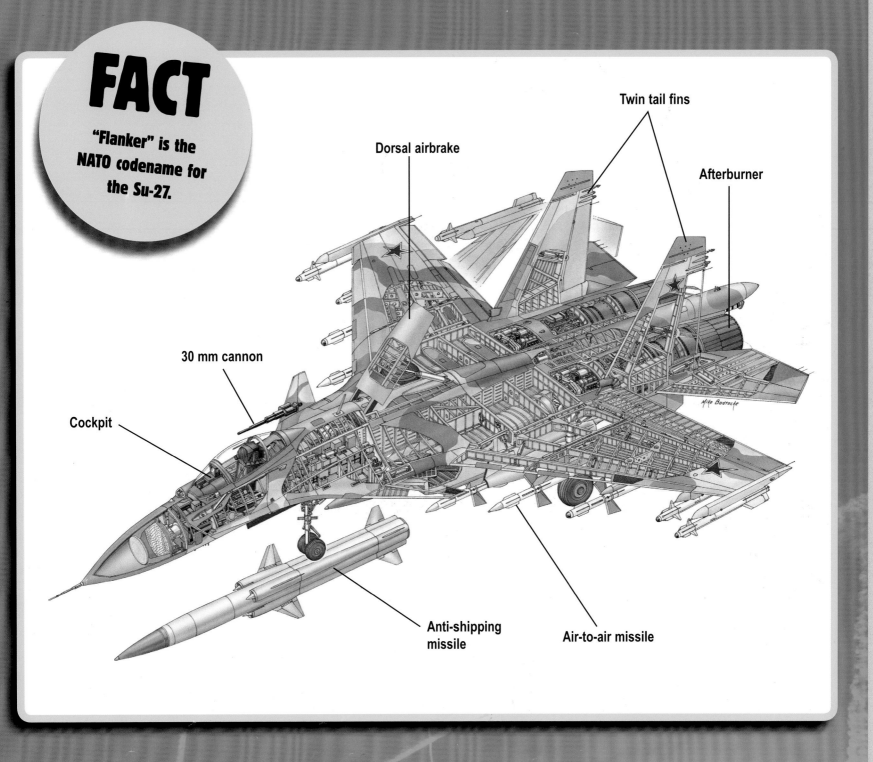

FACT

"Flanker" is the NATO codename for the Su-27.

Twin tail fins

Dorsal airbrake

Afterburner

30 mm cannon

Cockpit

Mike Badrocke

Anti-shipping missile

Air-to-air missile

JAS 39 Gripen

The Swedish aerospace company Saab first designed the JAS 39 Gripen fighter in 1979, to compete with Soviet warplanes. Introduced to the Swedish air force in 1997, the Gripen is still in service today.

During the **Cold War**, Sweden built up a powerful, modern air force. As an ally of NATO, Sweden had to be prepared for a possible Soviet invasion.

An Agile Air Force

Sweden's highways were built not only for automobiles but as landing and takeoff strips for military aircraft. In case of an invasion, Swedish planes could quickly **scramble** from road bases all over the country. The air force could not be destroyed with strikes on a few airfields. Because of this defensive strategy, the Gripen had to be specially designed to take off and land on snow-covered roadways.

This Gripen carries air-to-air missiles at its wing tips and two laser-guided bombs under each wing. A "drop tank" for extra fuel is below the fuselage.

Deadly Dogfighter

Saab developed the Gripen to replace the Saab 35 Draken and 37 Viggen. The Gripen is a multirole fighter with reconnaissance, air-to-air, and air-to-ground capabilities. Its excellent **aerodynamics**, Mach 2 speed (1,521 mph; 2,448 km/h), and **altitude** of 50,000 feet (15,240 m) make the Gripen deadly in a dogfight.

Did you know?

• *Gripen*, Swedish for "griffin," was the name chosen in a national vote. The griffin is a mythical beast with the head and wings of an eagle and the body of a lion.

• The air forces of the Czech Republic, Hungary, South Africa, and Thailand all use Gripens.

Its combat range is 500 miles (800 km). Weapons include a 27-mm (1.06-inch) cannon, laser-guided bombs, and air-to-air and air-to-ground missiles.

Gripen fighters fly in close formation. These are all one-seat models, with only a pilot, but the Gripen also has a JAS 39D model with a crew of two.

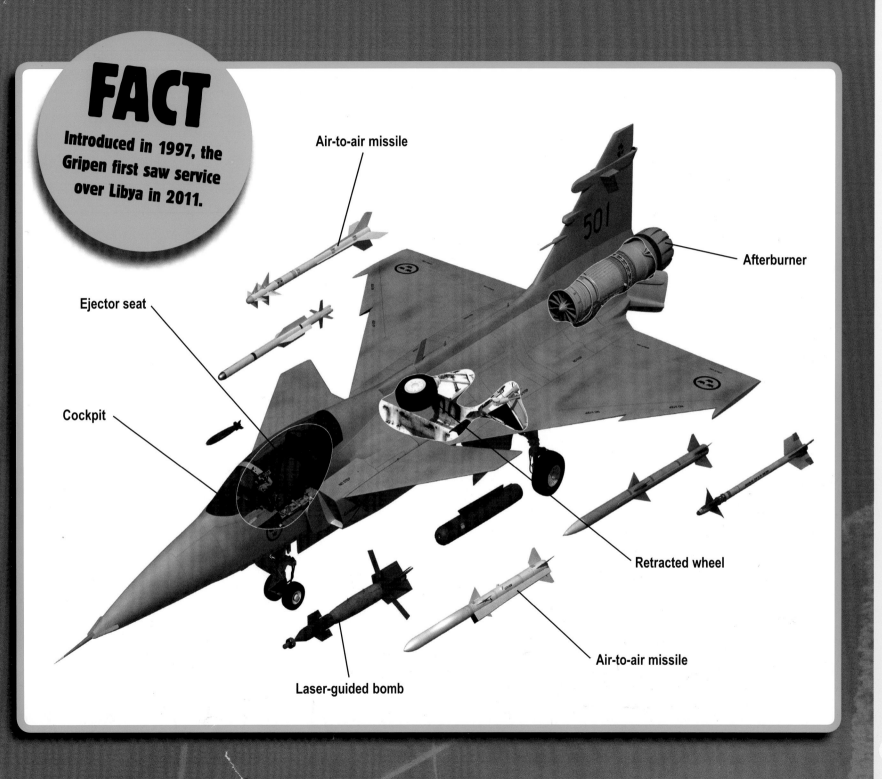

FACT

Introduced in 1997, the Gripen first saw service over Libya in 2011.

Air-to-air missile

Afterburner

Ejector seat

Cockpit

Retracted wheel

Air-to-air missile

Laser-guided bomb

F/A-18E/F Super Hornet

In 1983 the U.S. Navy introduced the multirole, all-weather F/A-18 Hornet, which operates from aircraft carriers around the world. The Hornet was among the first fighters developed both for dogfighting and air-to-ground strikes.

Although it has a limited combat range and weaponry, the F/A-18 Hornet's multirole capabilities have made it the Navy's most reliable plane.

Range, Speed, and Payload

Boeing's F/A-18E/F Super Hornet entered service in 1999 with an improved range of 1,467 miles (2,360 km) and a top speed of Mach 1.8—1,369 miles per hour (2,203 km/h). The larger Super Hornet has a wingspan of 44.9 feet (13.6 m), and an altitude

The pilot and flight officer are visible in this two-seat F/A-18F Super Hornet.

The afterburners of this single-seat U.S. Navy F/A-18E Super Hornet glow pink as it takes off from an aircraft carrier.

U.S. Navy replaced its Grumman F-14 Tomcat fighter with the Super Hornet, which now serves together with the original Hornet. The Marines have not yet adopted any of the 500 Super Hornets built so far.

limit of 50,000 feet (15,240 m). Its weapons include a 20-mm (0.79-inch) gun, air-to-air and air-to-surface missiles, and laser-guided bombs.

Into Combat

The Super Hornet flew its first combat mission in 2002 and has seen action in Iraq, Afghanistan, and against pirates off the coast of Somalia. The U.S. Navy and Marine Corps—and the militaries of seven foreign nations—fly F/A-18 Hornets. Only Australia has so far ordered the Super Hornet. The

Did you know?

• • • • • • • • • • • • • • • • •

• Because of its superior aerodynamics, the Hornet is the plane of choice for the Navy's flight demonstration squadron, the Blue Angels.

• With five external fuel tanks, the Super Hornet can also serve as an **airborne tanker** to refuel another plane in the air.

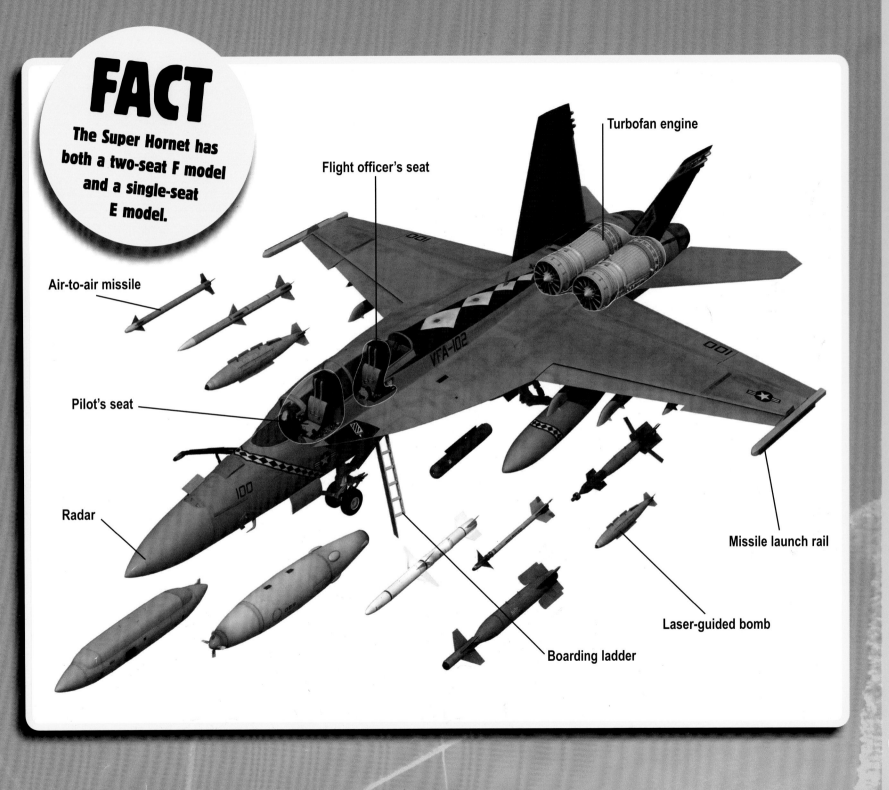

FACT
The Super Hornet has both a two-seat F model and a single-seat E model.

Turbofan engine

Flight officer's seat

Air-to-air missile

Pilot's seat

Radar

Missile launch rail

Laser-guided bomb

Boarding ladder

VFA-102

100

Eurofighter Typhoon

NATO allies Britain, France, and Germany began development of an advanced multirole fighter in the 1980s to counter the Soviet Su-27 and MiG-29. They wanted a similar advanced fighter for air-to-air combat.

• • • • • • • • • • • • •

Disagreements delayed the fighter project. France wanted a fighter that could take off from an aircraft carrier and soon withdrew from the program to build its own Dassault Rafale.

A Modern European Fighter

NATO allies Spain and Italy joined Britain and Germany in the fighter development program in 1983. Then the fall of the Soviet Union in 1991 ended the Cold War threat. There was less of a need for European fighters. Still, these countries had made a big investment in the project, and they did not want to rely only on American fighters. The Eurofighter Typhoon was finally introduced in 2003.

A German Typhoon's drag parachute works along with its brakes to slow the airplane down after landing.

The fins behind the nose of this Typhoon are designed for stability and to help control the plane.

of 1,800 miles (2,900 km). Armed with a 27-mm (1.06-inch) cannon, the Typhoon can carry air-to-air missiles, air-to-surface missiles, and laser-guided bombs.

Quick and Powerful

The Typhoon is an effective strike fighter. With its 36-foot (11 m) delta wing it is also highly maneuverable and effective in close air-to-air combat. The aircraft can climb to 55,000 feet (16,764 m) with a maximum speed of Mach 2 (1,521 mph; 2,448 km/h). Typhoons have a range

Did you know?

• In 2010 the British and German air forces "grounded" their Typhoons (not allowing them to fly) while they investigated problems with the plane's ejection seat.

• More than 390 Typhoons are active in the air forces of Britain, Germany, Spain, Italy, Austria, and Saudi Arabia.

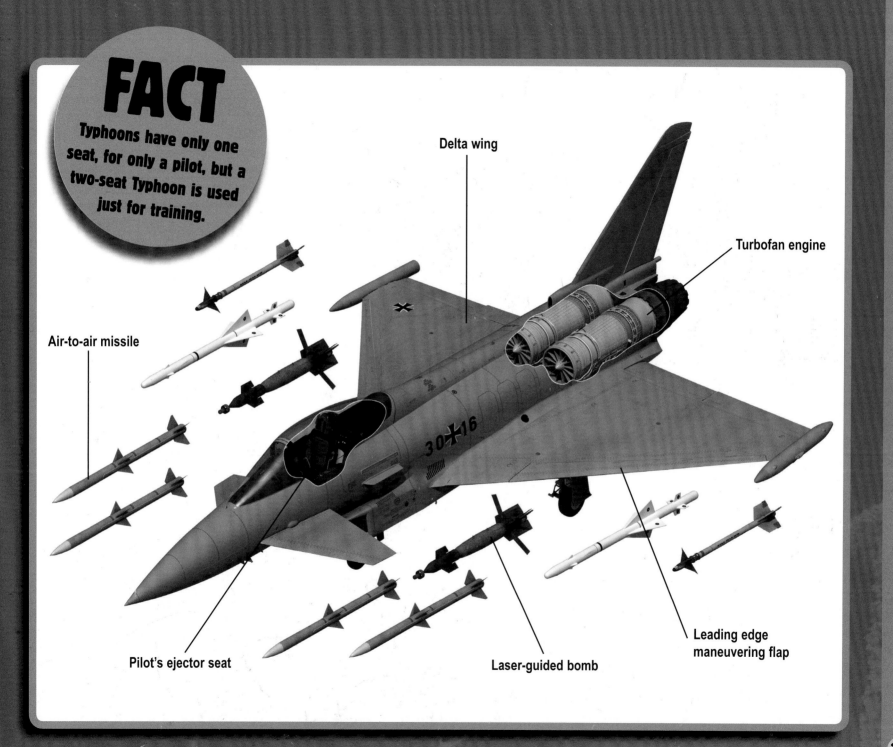

FACT

Typhoons have only one seat, for only a pilot, but a two-seat Typhoon is used just for training.

Delta wing

Turbofan engine

Air-to-air missile

Pilot's ejector seat

Laser-guided bomb

Leading edge maneuvering flap

30+16

Dassault Rafale

In the late 1970s, both France's air force and navy were ready to replace their fighters, which had been in service since the 1950s. They wanted an agile, multirole warplane.

Dassault Aviation designed the Rafale for air-to-air and air-to-ground combat, and also for aircraft-carrier operations. The delta-wing Rafale had the latest computer and radar technology.

A Blast of Wind

In French, "rafale" means a blast of wind. The first Rafale flight took place in 1986, and in 2001 the warplane was introduced into the French military. Dassault built 122 Rafales.

Rafales are armed with air-to-surface and air-to-air missiles, and bombs. Just behind the pilot's cockpit are foreplanes: fins for flight control and stability.

Did you know?

• **The delta-wing design gives an aircraft high maneuverability and is stronger than the swept-back wing design.**

• **Delta wings are easier (and cost less) to manufacture. Also, fuel and other equipment can be stored in the space inside the wings.**

Rafales have seen action in Africa many times. In 2011, Rafales took part in France's operations in support of anti-government forces in Libya. In 2013 Rafale aircraft helped French troops defeat rebels in Mali.

A Rafale patrols over a desert region. The large cigar-shaped units under the wings are extra fuel tanks.

Combat Over Land or Sea

The twin-engine, single-seat Rafale can carry a variety of armaments. These include air-to-air and air-to-ground missiles, and bombs ranging from 275 pounds (125 kg) to 2,200 pounds (1,000 kg). The Rafale can also be armed with anti-ship or nuclear missiles. The Rafale's wingspan is 35.4 feet (10.8 m), and its top speed is Mach 1.8 (1,369 mph; 2,203 km/h). Its range is 2,300 miles (3,700 km) and top altitude is 50,000 feet (15,235 m).

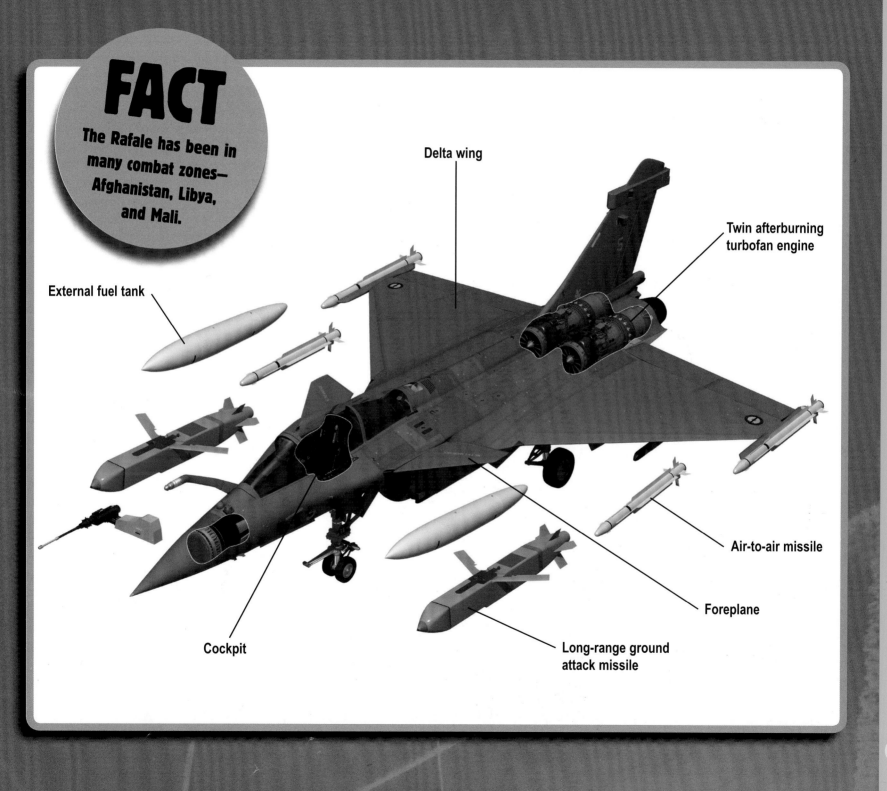

FACT

The Rafale has been in many combat zones—Afghanistan, Libya, and Mali.

Delta wing

Twin afterburning turbofan engine

External fuel tank

Air-to-air missile

Foreplane

Cockpit

Long-range ground attack missile

F-22 Raptor

The Russians built the Fulcrum fighter in the 1980s, so the U.S. Air Force wanted to upgrade its own fighter fleet. The F-22 Raptor was designed to outperform the Fulcrum.

The Raptor has advanced electronics and flight controls, and improved **stealth** features. Built for air-to-air combat, this fighter was to give the U.S. Air Force control of the skies.

Advanced Technology

The single-seat F-22 Raptor has a greater **climb rate** than older U.S. fighters. The Raptor's advanced computer technology, design, and special coatings make it difficult for enemy radar to find and target it.

The F-22's stealth and advanced air-combat features give its pilots "first-shot" advantage over enemy warplanes.

Lockheed Martin, the main contractor, built 195 Raptors from 1996 to 2011. To build one F-22, it took a thousand companies (supplying materials and equipment) and 95,000 workers.

F-22 Raptors turn above Virginia's Langley Air Force Base, where they are part of the 94th Fighter Squadron.

Did you know?

• Federal law bars the sale of the F-22 Raptor to foreign countries. This is to prevent its advanced technology from being studied and copied.

• The Raptor F-22 was introduced in 2005, but the F-35 Lighting II fighter was already planned to replace it.

Speed: Mach 2.25

The span of the Raptor's swept-back wings is 44 feet 6 inches (13.6 m). Estimated top speed is Mach 2.25—1,711 miles per hour (2,754 km/h) and its range is 1,840 miles (2,754 km) with two external fuel tanks mounted. The F-22 can climb to 65,000 feet (19,812 m). It carries a 20-mm (0.79-inch) cannon and is armed with air-to-air and air-to-ground missiles or bombs. Most Raptors are stationed in the United States. Some are based in the Middle East, but none have seen action yet.

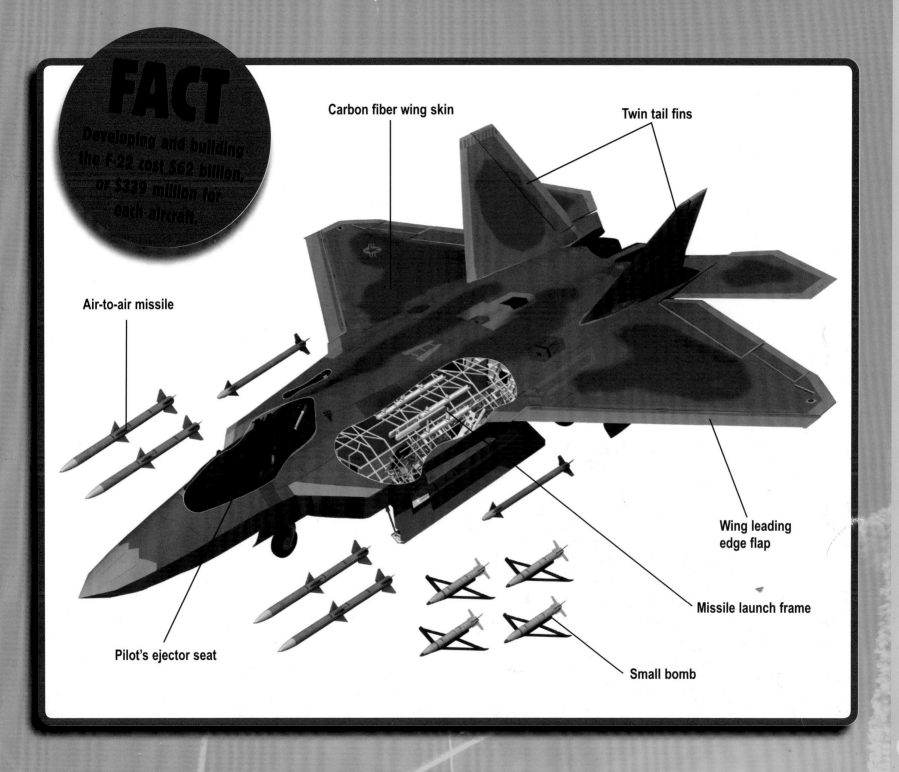

FACT

Developing and building the F-22 cost $62 billion, or $339 million for each aircraft.

Carbon fiber wing skin

Twin tail fins

Air-to-air missile

Wing leading edge flap

Missile launch frame

Pilot's ejector seat

Small bomb

F-35 Lightning II

To replace the many fighters that are more than 30 years old, the U.S. military is developing the F-35 as the most high-tech stealth fighter ever to take to the skies.

After 10 years in production and $400 billion spent, however, the F-35 is not yet fully operational. The reasons include performance and safety problems and huge cost-overruns.

The Main U.S. Fighter

Although early work on the F-35 Lightning II began in 1996, it will not be ready for service until at least 2015. Hundreds of problems with equipment, computer software, engine, structure, and design have slowed production and increased costs. The Pentagon wants more than 2,400 F-35s, which would make it America's main **tactical aircraft**. The F-35 is difficult for

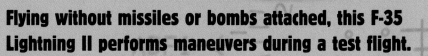

Flying without missiles or bombs attached, this F-35 Lightning II performs maneuvers during a test flight.

vertically, like a helicopter). A third type operates from aircraft carriers. The F-35 will climb to 60,000 feet (18,288 m) and have a range of 1,365 miles (2,200 km).

ground-based radar to detect, and the fighter's electronic warfare systems can see enemy aircraft before they spot the F-35.

A Design for Many Roles

The single-seat F-35 is termed a "joint strike fighter" because it is designed for the Air Force, Navy, and Marine Corps. This fighter has three models: one for normal takeoff and landing and another for short takeoff and landing (including

Did you know?

• At $161 million each, the F-35 Lighting II is one of the most expensive weapons the United States has ever developed.

• Other countries have ordered F-35s, including the United Kingdom and Japan. Delays and increased costs, however, are making some buyers change their minds.

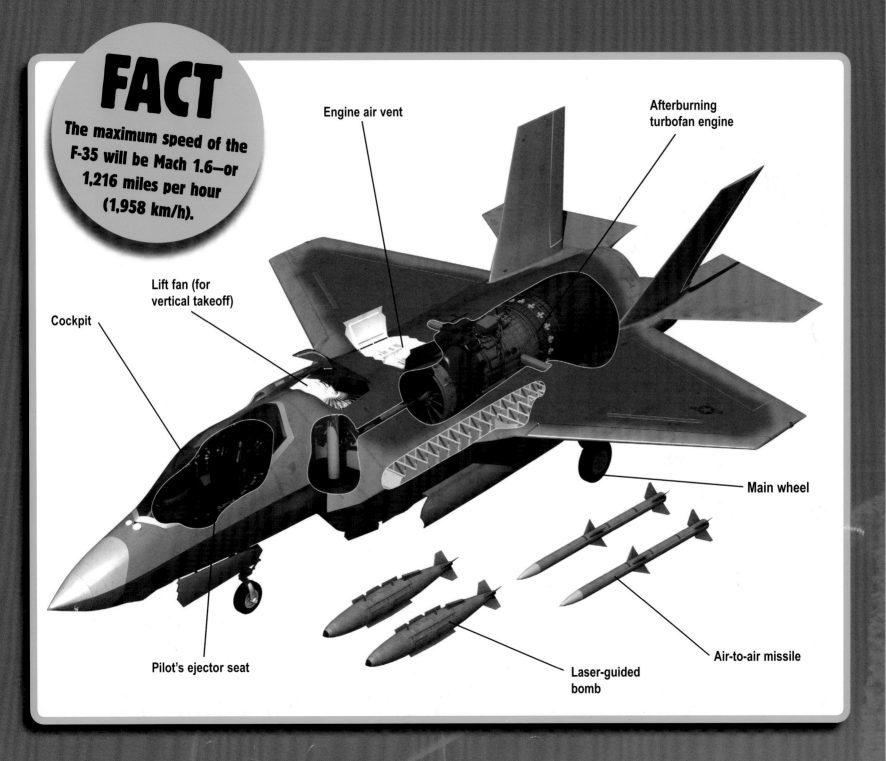

FACT

The maximum speed of the F-35 will be Mach 1.6—or 1,216 miles per hour (1,958 km/h).

Engine air vent

Afterburning turbofan engine

Lift fan (for vertical takeoff)

Cockpit

Main wheel

Pilot's ejector seat

Laser-guided bomb

Air-to-air missile

Glossary

aerodynamics — the way in which air interacts with a solid object moving through it, such as an airplane's wing

agility — the ability to move easily, nimbly, quickly

air superiority — having the advantage in air combat

air-to-air combat — a fight between opposing aircraft

airborne tanker — a plane used to refuel another plane during flight

aircraft carrier — a warship that is a base for aircraft

altitude — height above the ground

anti-ship — can destroy a ship

climb rate — the vertical speed of an aircraft, or the rate of change in altitude

Cold War — a period from 1947 to 1990 when the Soviet Union and its allies had a military standoff with U.S.-led countries

conventional — weaponry that is not nuclear

counter — to act against

delta wing — an aircraft's single triangular wing

escort — fighters sent to accompany and protect other aircraft, such as bombers, on flight missions

fighter — a high-speed, maneuverable military aircraft armed to destroy other aircraft

foreplane — a horizontal surface positioned between the nose and the main wing of an aircraft to help with stability and flight control

fuselage — the main body of an aircraft

interceptor — a high-speed fighter whose goal is to destroy enemy aircraft

laser-guided — when a laser is used to mark a target, then a bomb or missile follows the laser beam in order to hit the target

Mach — a number that represents the ratio of the speed of an aircraft to the speed of sound (an airplane traveling Mach 1 is traveling at the speed of sound; Mach 2 would be twice the speed of sound, and so on)

multirole fighter — a fighter plane that has more than one purpose

NATO — a defense alliance between the United States, Canada, and many European countries

nuclear — weapons that get their destructive power from the energy that is released by an uncontrolled nuclear reaction

scramble — when aircraft receive an alert to take off immediately in order to intercept enemy aircraft

stealth — an aircraft designed using technology that makes it difficult to detect using sonar or radar

strike fighter — a fighter plane that is used mainly to attack ground targets, but which can also fight in air-to-air combat

supermaneuverable — a type of aircraft that can perform maneuvers that are impossible using regular aerodynamic controls, including flying very slowly and quickly regaining control of the aircraft if it stalls

supersonic — faster than the speed of sound

swept-back wings — wings that are not straight, but swept back

tactical aircraft — aircraft used to support military and naval operations both on the ground and at sea

Index